HIGH JOELTAGE

101 JOElts for Becoming Amazingly Effective

Joe M. Turner

TurnerMagic Publications

Copyright © 2012 Joe M. Turner

All rights reserved.

ISBN-13: 978-0615728551

ISBN-10: 0615728553

TurnerMagic Publications
2870 Peachtree Road NW
Suite 436
Atlanta, GA 30305
United States of America

DEDICATION

For Hayley and Preston
and especially for Rosemary

CONTENTS

Acknowledgments	i
Author's Note	1
What Is a JOElt?	2
101 JOElts	3
Amazing Networking	40
About the Author	49

ACKNOWLEDGMENTS

To the parents, grandparents,
aunts and uncles,
teachers, professors, and mentors
who loved, taught and guided…

To the managers, partners, owners,
executive and senior vice presidents,
clients, customers, colleagues,
and networking buddies
who led and inspired…

To the fellow speakers and performers
who have encouraged and contributed to my work
both on the platform and in this book…

Thank you.

AUTHOR'S NOTE

We all have an audience.

The audience may change – it could be prospects or customers one day and vendors the next. It could be students or trainees on Monday and instructors on Friday. It could be your direct reports in the morning and your supervisors in the afternoon. But whatever you do, you always have an audience.

Whoever your audience is, every interaction they have with you is an opportunity to energize and amaze them. Every time they interact with your personal or professional brand, you have a chance to create a powerful impression that sets the stage for future success.

This short book is a collection of tips and ideas that have helped me grow my personal brand as well as my business brand. Whether dealing with improving personal effectiveness, deepening business skills, or simply provoking a positive thought, the ultimate goal of all of these ideas is to help you have an amazing impact on your audience.

Go amaze someone.

Joe M. Turner
November 2012

WHAT IS A JOELT?

jolt : v. 1. To move or strike with a sudden impact: He jolted his opponent with a heavy punch.
2. To make suddenly active or effective: The remark jolted my memory.

n. 1. A sudden jarring as from a heavy blow, an abrupt movement, or a collision.
2. A brief, strong portion: a jolt of electricity; a jolt of strong cider.

JOElt : n. A burst of insight, motivation, or action as delivered by Joe M. Turner, either in writing or in a live presentation.

JOEltage : n. The cumulative impact of multiple JOElts on an individual's brain, brand, or business.

101 JOELTS

1

The audience wants you to succeed. Whether they're in a theatre, a convention hall, your retail store, or visiting your web site, they want you, your products, or your services to be fantastic. They want a story they can tell others; something to make their friends jealous and sorry that they missed. Give them that story.

2

You know the old saying that nobody knows what the future holds? That is an excuse we use to distract ourselves from a truth that is both frightening and empowering: tomorrow holds the consequences of today's decisions. There will also be some random elements in the mix, but a large part of the future is very easy to foresee in reasonable detail.

The future holds the results of the actions we take now.

3

Your expertise is not amazing anyone as long as it's unexpressed. Capture it in a shareable form regularly. Get it out of your head and into the universe.

Hat tip: Melissa Galt, Prosper by Design, www.melissagalt.com

4

Most of us saw some amazing science demonstrations in school when we were kids. Did you ever see a flower shatter like glass after being immersed in liquid nitrogen? Maybe you saw a ping pong ball floating in a column of blowing air, refusing to fall even when tipped at an angle. If you ever saw a partial eclipse of the sun through a pinhole camera or even projected on the ground through the leaves of a tree, you'll never forget it.

Most of these experiments were amazing because we were seeing familiar objects behaving in unfamiliar ways. Even though the results were obviously possible, they were unusual because they were not the normal, expected behavior of those objects. Flowers don't shatter. Balls don't levitate. The sun doesn't look like part of it has been bitten off. When things around you don't behave as expected, you are well on your way to experiencing amazement.

If you wish to amaze, you must act in ways that are possible but not expected. Don't behave randomly, but rather make an unexpected move in a calculated way that emphasizes some property or characteristic of your brand that you believe is a strategic advantage. Amazing experiences are by definition outside the norm.

5

Look at your business processes. Find the most trivial or boring interaction you have with your audience. Hide a pleasant surprise in that process and that amazing experience will be a topic of conversation for a long time.

If you want them to talk about you, give them something to talk about.

6

Learn from the design concept of negative space: you can be amazing for what you don't do. You know that marketing thing you do that everyone else in your space is doing? That's a good place to start. Cut it out, turn it completely upside down, or do the exact opposite. Be the FedEx arrow.

7

Be amazing to look at. If you can't hire an image consultant, start by getting some coaching from people whose look you admire.

8

Your grandmother probably didn't use email or social media, but she did know to send out a thank you note. Want to amaze someone in a world of high-tech noise? Send a handwritten card or letter, or at least a personalized one via a service like Send Out Cards.

Put a physical point of contact into their largely virtual world and you will be remembered.

9

"Sing out, Louise!"
– Mama Rose (from the musical Gypsy)

You will not amaze people with your eyes constantly looking at the ground. Stand up straight, shoulders back, voice strong, making strong eye contact. Speak up. If there's a microphone, don't be afraid of it. Use it. Even if you think your voice is strong enough, use it.

10

Amaze by turning common experiences into uncommon pleasures. Get your business card professionally designed and put something on it that invites comment or question. A random photo, the newest techie widget, a quote from your favorite Shakespearian work, or just a blank line to fill in with something you create for them right there on the spot.

Put something there that sparks a pleasant recollection of your meeting.

11

The overt demonstration of expertise is one way to amaze. Capture the questions that your clients and prospects ask about your business. Answer them in blog post and article form, then push that out through your social media.

12

Be careful what you don't wish for, because you may never get it.

13

We live in a society where honesty is often an amazing breath of fresh air. People are often jaded and conditioned to expect the worst. Embrace your real expertise, deliver real value, and choose the honest path. When your business and your life are congruent with your ideals, people notice. (Caveat: People also notice when they aren't.)

14

Ever heard that rules were made to be broken? That's a recipe for disaster. In the plural, breaking "the rules" is a pathway to hardship. But breaking one rule? That's a different proposition altogether.

Look for one assumption about the way business is done in your space, and thoughtfully contradict it.

15

The best rules to break are the ones people don't even recognize as rules. Those assumptions are a fertile field for growth.

16

Quick – right now – look at your calendar for one year ago today. Go into your email archive or documents folder for a year ago. Make contact this week with every client you touched during that week. Use a note, a postcard, or phone call. Only use email or an e-card as a last resort.

Do it now.

17

"A lot of times, people don't know what they want until you show it to them."
— Steve Jobs (Business Week, May 12, 1998)

While there's no substitute for doing your market research and taking time to know and understand your clients, don't get so bogged down in what makes them customers that you forget what makes you a provider. Create real value and you'll create demand.

18

Most people and most businesses are coasting. Most people spend more time on autopilot than in conscious decision-making. You can begin your transformation into an amazing person or business simply by being one of the few who put in some actual effort beyond what's expected.

19

Canadian magician Jay Sankey teaches that his magic became more amazing to his audiences when he realized that as he performs, each observer collects and remembers a series of images. Sankey took time to decide what he wanted those images to be, then choreographed his performances so that those "freeze frame" moments received the greatest focus.

In your business processes, are you calling attention to the moments you want your audience to remember? Or are you leaving the decision up to random chance? Do you think random chance will support your brand's lasting impact better than your own choices?

20

Dai Vernon, the iconic performer and teacher whom magicians worldwide still revere as "the Professor" twenty years after his death, famously said that "Confusion is not magic." His point is that a muddled presentation of a mixture of effects will not create a pleasing experience of the impossible in a spectator's mind.

Amazement requires a number of conditions, one of which is clarity. The production of four aces from thin air is amazing, but it's much less so if it happens without context or purpose during a coin trick. When you package your products and services, don't throw aces into your coin routine. Rather than adding value, it diminishes the amazement value of both experiences.

21

As you progress toward your goal, you will find obstacles in your path. Events happen. Circumstances arise. People show up with alternate or conflicting goals.

It is a popular cliché to suggest that through singularly focused vision, heartfelt mantras, and chanted affirmations, we can simply go on acting as if the obstacles were not actually there. The truth is that sometimes we don't get to choose where other things or people stand. We do, however, get to choose our path.

Amazing people are not blind to obstacles. They just choose not to be blinded by them. Don't chant or affirm yourself into pretending that the obstacle isn't there. Instead, exercise your very real ability to overcome it.

22

Because most people live on autopilot, you can amaze a great many with your incredible foresight simply by paying attention to what is happening around you and making common sense deductions.

23

At least once a day, notice a small but pleasant detail about two people you encounter: someone you know, and someone you don't. Comment positively on it. This simple act, if cultivated into a habit, will not only change the way others perceive you, but also the way you perceive others. Your ability to communicate with other people will be transformed by this change in attitude.

24

"A creative man is motivated by the desire to achieve, not by the desire to beat others."
— Ayn Rand

The times when I have felt most profoundly hopeless were the times when my thoughts were most focused on measuring myself compared to others' achievements instead of my own goals. Measure your progress in relation to your own yesterday, not someone else's today. You will amaze yourself and others when you grant yourself that freedom.

25

Don't mistake confidence and focus for egotism. Likewise, don't mistake fear or indecision for humility.

26

Don't downplay the importance of good public relations and well-developed soft skills. Someone will have to be the most amazing person nobody ever heard of, but don't let it be you. It's not about being famous. It's about multiplying the impact of your efforts.

27

Amaze through failure by learning from the error, adapting your approach, and trying again. Persistence is amazing because it is extraordinary.

28

Having trouble coming up with that amazing idea? Define more boundaries. It is a mistake to think that creativity is solely a function of having no limits or coloring outside the lines. Those lines are on a page so that the crayon has something to mark. The canvas, the stage, and the instrument each have a defined size or range.

The artist with no boundaries is an artist with no medium and ultimately, no art. The leader with no boundaries is a leader with no real vision and ultimately, no achievement.

29

Make it a habit to dress slightly better than most others at the events you attend. This will increase the perceived value of your services and magnify the impact that you have on the people in the group.

30

*"You cannot dream yourself into a character;
you must hammer and forge yourself into one."*
— Henry David Thoreau

Dreaming, wishing, visualizing, chanting, meditating, affirming, and even detailed work planning are all well and good, but don't wait for the universe to take action on your behalf. It's not going to happen until you actually do something. Execute. Amazing requires action.

31

Launching a creative project is like launching a rocket. In art, as in physics, you ultimately need something for the motivating force to push against. The same holds true in business — you can't be everything to anyone, but you can be something to everyone. You need a defined problem to push against.

Enjoy the paradox that in the context of creativity, some constraints can actually be freeing rather than confining.

32

Respect other people's time. You will astound a jaded, disillusioned population by confirming appointments in advance, checking in with them if you are detained for some reason, and following up on meetings and tasks as agreed.

It sounds easy, but the real-world results prove that it isn't easy at all. Does everyone you know do these things? Do you? Start by amazing one person this week with your respect for his or her time.

33

The equally amazing corollary to committing to respecting other people's time is that your personal productivity and use of your own time will necessarily improve. The better you manage your impact on other people's time, the better you manage your own.

34

My high school band director used to say, "Get your head out of the music and get the music in your head." We were so focused on reading notes on the page that we weren't watching her conduct. Result? Poor tempo, poor dynamics, and a lack of cohesion regardless of whether the correct notes were played.

The notes are on the page for a reason, but the sheet music is not the music. The tasks you perform, the tools you use, and the processes you lead are not your job. Your job is to create an amazing experience for your audience.

35

For centuries, books on magic have traditionally used the "Effect/Method" format to teach illusions. The opening part of a trick's description is a clear explanation of the effect; that is, what exactly does an audience member experience when witnessing the performance?

The method comes next, explaining a way to achieve that effect. One great secret of magic is that for any given effect, there are usually dozens of methods. You can amaze with a great new method, but legends are born from new effects.

36

*"A ship is safe in a harbor, but harbors are not
what ships are made for."*
– quoted often by Rear Admiral Grace Hopper

Generally speaking, a ship anchored in a harbor is amazing either because of where it's going or because of where it's been. Those that are going somewhere won't be sticking around for long – they have work to do. Those who achieved amazingness because of where they've been are usually anxious to find a new mission – either in action, in training, or as a lasting tribute to great deeds.

No ship is ever truly amazing for having stayed in harbor while other ships went out into the world. Ships are amazing for what happens outside the harbor.

37

Amazing is both a verb and an adjective. Either way, this statement is true: A taste for amazing, once acquired, is not easily lost. Don't miss an opportunity to intensify your taste for the verb; don't miss a chance to feed your audience's taste for the adjective.

38

Fortune favors the bold – sometimes with success, and sometimes with a lesson in discerning when to be more patient.

When the variables concerning your success are predominantly within your control, be bold. When the variables are mostly controlled by someone or something else, be patient.

39

Highly developed skill, committed preparation, and precise execution aren't magic. They just look like it to those who aren't doing them.

40

Declare victory over some issue or situation every day. Break things down as small as you need to go in order to find something where you can say, "I won."

41

Let your team see you engage in both skill-building and delegation. Amazing performers play to their strengths and outsource what slows them down. Model continuous improvement as well as willingness to get needed help.

42

Laurel & Hardy. Abbott & Costello. Burns & Allen. C3PO & R2D2. Penn & Teller.

Amazingness sometimes shows up dressed as an ampersand. Be vigilant for effective partnerships; sometimes they are so effective that they redefine both partners.

43

Research. Listen. Decide. Adjust. Don't get hung up on step 3 - that's why step 4 is there. Being amazing requires decision and action. You can tweak it later.

44

You achieve the state of amazing one stunning moment at a time. If everything is a priority, then nothing is a priority. Pick something. Rehearse it, perfect it, and perform it.

45

"Son, you just paid the looking price. Lessons are extra."
– Lancey Howard (from the film The Cincinnati Kid*)*

In the classic film *The Cincinnati Kid*, Edward G. Robinson's character Lancey Howard speaks this line to a gambler whom he has just beaten at poker. The gambler asks Lancey how he beat him. Lancey refuses to tell him. Why? Greed? Power? Something else?

As I see it, Lancey wasn't being merely greedy or stingy or power hungry. Whichever of those factors may have been present, I think he could also tell from the other man's play that he wasn't ready to comprehend or apply what Lancey would have to share in order to explain his victory. Just as in magic, there is a lot of difference between knowing that something is possible and knowing how something is done. There is yet another gap between knowing how something it done and actually being able to do it.

The way we play for the penny-ante pots always signals to the observant expert whether we're ready for more advanced knowledge. The amazing performer doesn't need a million-dollar pot in order to demonstrate million-dollar expertise.

46

It's true – to get amazing results, luck is part of the game. Fortunately, L.U.C.K. can be manufactured.

47

L.U.C.K. - Step 1: Lock and load. Get your target clearly in mind and do whatever it takes to be ready to pull the trigger at the exact moment required.

48

L.U.C.K. – Step 2: Unrelenting effort. Every attempt gets a full throttle effort. There are no practice runs. There may be research and development, but even those attempts get total focus and effort.

49

L.U.C.K. – Step 3: Continuously improve. Each attempt always offers insight into what must happen next. Don't miss the opportunity to learn from your own experiences as well as those of others.

50

L.U.C.K. – Step 4: Keep on keeping on. Keep doing, keep going, keep trying, keep learning.

Some people get there on the first try, but they are statistically negligible which is something you don't want to be. Besides, the adversity will make the movie about your success much more interesting.

51

It may be better to be lucky than good, but why choose? Amazing people are lucky *and* good.

52

Amazing performers rehearse tirelessly but are adept at creating "the illusion of the first time." If you want to be amazing, think of contingencies, prepare your ad-libs, and deliver them as if they simply occurred to you on the spot.

53

Here's another secret about the most amazing performers: if something happens in the show and the perfect ad lib comes to them on the spot, or if someone in the audience throws out an amazing line, the moment is not forgotten or lost. The amazing performer records and uses the line again, and may even go so far as to restructure his or her show to ensure that the opportunity to use that line is replicated in all future performances.

Here's the amazing tip: don't lose those gems. A long career produces plenty of them; an amazing career builds amazing experiences with them.

54

Change for the sake of change is not necessarily a positive thing. Change derives value from its direction and destination, not from its motion.

Choose to be amazing for where you're going and for what you're accomplishing along the way, not for the amount of unfocused effort you can waste in getting there.

55

Which phase are you in?

Like a liquid, most individuals and organizations inevitably drift toward the path of least resistance. Like a gas, most expenses and processes will expand to fill all the available space. Like a solid, many great brands and companies get so heavy and dense that they sink to the bottom of the river they were navigating, only moving when the force of the current is enough to nudge them along the river's floor, never again seeing the twists and turns that are coming. (Even business tips can be made amazing when framed as unexpected metaphors!)

Want to amaze your audience? Think about how your brand relates to something completely unrelated to your industry. Those similarities and differences will spark insights that you would be less likely to have when thinking in your familiar patterns.

Amazing people don't just see relationships between unrelated things; they actively look for them and leverage them to spark creativity.

56

Amazing isn't something you can be until it's something you can do. Focus on the verb, and the adjective will take care of itself.

57

The most amazing and influential personal branding doesn't come from having an elevator speech. It comes from living an elevated life.

58

"Do I contradict myself?
Very well, then I contradict myself.
I am large, I contain multitudes."
— Walt Whitman, "Song of Myself"

The amazing person remembers that a tip can be exactly, perfectly right on Monday and yet may be exactly, perfectly, completely wrong by Tuesday. Only a leader who is operating "in the moment" can make the call.

Accept the fact that you might have to change your approach and contradict what you thought and did yesterday. It is not flippant, flighty, or indicative of a lack of core values to adapt your tactics to changing circumstances.

Amazing people know the difference between being steadfast and being stubborn.

59

Want to be an amazing communicator? When you tell your story, give *details*. Don't just hint about your mistake, grief, embarrassment, sickness, or hurt. Share what you learned in it and how you grew through it. The audience will be amazed at your honesty. You'll connect with their humanity. They will trust you.

Hat tip: Janie Walters, Champion Communications, www.janiewalters.com

60

"I am constantly amazed at how stupid I was two weeks ago."
– Alan Weiss, Million Dollar Consulting

This quip is a great example of exaggerated self-deprecation shining a light on the importance of continuous improvement. Obviously Alan Weiss wasn't stupid two weeks ago. What he is saying is that in the last two weeks he believes he has introduced himself to enough new data and new ideas that he could have improved decisions made only a couple of weeks earlier.

There are many lessons here. First, Weiss is making decisions, constantly, and taking action. Many of us don't feel the impact of new information on our decisions because we haven't made any important ones recently. Second, he is constantly reading, listening, and working through new ideas. He actively seeks out a constant stream of new ideas.

Want to be amazing? Take action, and keep learning.

61

Sometimes the alternate route turns out to be better than the way you thought you wanted to go. Don't curse the detour so much that you forget to observe the new scenery and make notes about the resources and benefits the new route offers.

62

It's a good idea to try the local beer. It's also a good idea to think of three other ways that suggestion – getting a taste of "going native" – could be applied to other areas of your life and work. Give that a go right now.

63

Magicians and other performers have long appreciated the wisdom of finding and cherishing a place to be bad. Everyone needs a lab to work out the new material. Don't abuse that audience by showing them dreck. You should still take them material you have thoughtfully prepared and rehearsed, even though you don't yet know whether it will be A-material or B-material.

If you have the ability to do this lab testing under a different brand, consider that carefully. If, like many performers, you are your brand and can't really hide that, try to find a lab where the audience is limited and regular. You can develop relationships in that kind of place that will transcend any hiccups. For magicians, this might be a restaurant or bar. For musicians, it might be a favorite off-the-beaten-path club. For other entrepreneurs, this might be a trusted collection of networking colleagues.

Find and cherish a place to be bad. The ability to go from rehearsal to preview in a trusted environment is an immensely helpful asset in a journey to amazingness.

64

Amaze yourself. Order something different on the menu. Take a different route home. Read or listen to a different genre. Change, not for the sake of change, but for the sake of cultivating appreciation, comfort, and skill with the process.

If you've intentionally built up your change muscles, you'll be better prepared to handle unexpected changes when they inevitably happen.

65

W.C. Fields. Lucille Ball. Howard Cosell. Phyllis Diller. Jimmy Durante. Beatrice Arthur. Louis Armstrong.

It's not about having the prettiest voice, the most sonorous voice, the voice with the biggest range, best resonance, or even the most distinct enunciation. Sometimes amazingness is found by making a feature or an asset out of what others would consider a flaw or an aberration. Fields could never have been a Gable or a Bogart. But they could never have been a Fields.

Amaze by emphasizing whatever you've got that the others don't. Build your value proposition around that. Your voice doesn't have to be the prettiest – it just has to be yours.

66

The magical icon Dai Vernon once lamented that "Magicians stop thinking too soon." After an intense search to find a working method to achieve a desired effect, most magicians stop looking and in the process, fail to consider that there might be a better way. Another performer will often pick up the ball and run with it, ultimately getting credit for finding the ideal method that escaped the first performer's discovery simply because he stopped thinking too soon.

Amazing people keep thinking after a solution is found. They run through the tape. They push a little harder even though victory has already been achieved. Don't let moderate success distract you from the even greater achievement right around the corner.

67

By and large, sweetened iced tea seems much sweeter now than it used to be. It seems like every place wants to out-sweeten the others. Even my grandmother's brewed-on-the-stove sweet tea, sweetened with heaping scoops of cane sugar, wasn't as sweet as some of the syrup I am served today.

Are you serving syrup? Have you allowed your product lines, service offerings, or even your operational processes to fall into the "wait, we can make it sweeter" cycle?

The amazing leader knows to pull back to ordering "half and half" for two great reasons. First, the taste is restored to what was desired and is not merely a version of what everyone else is serving and drinking. Second, there is positive differentiation to be had by being the first to start the new trend of ordering or offering "half and half."

Amazing people find the balance point between being responsive and being reactive. Call it the "sweet spot" if you must, but not too sweet!

68

Laugh! On the average, adults laugh only seven times a day compared to over 300 times a day for kids! Laughter can produce positive results for your team and workplace.

Try starting your next staff meeting with a joke, a paper airplane contest or "the funniest thing I've seen in the workplace" question. You will be amazed at the results from including lots of laughter in the work day!

Hat tip: Dianne Dyar, Dyar Communication + Strategy, www.diannedyar.com

69

I once witnessed a young stage illusionist performing at a convention. It was all glass and chrome and smoke machines, and the only thing bigger than the props was the young man's ego.

In the course of a few poorly performed routines, the young man demonstrated a complete lack of understanding of human beings. When he had to move something on the stage, he commented that the stagehands had gotten the placement of the props wrong. When a sound cue was late, he made a lame joke at the expense of the sound tech. Within a few minutes of his troubles beginning he had managed to alienate not just the audience, but also the entire crew who were backstage making his performance possible.

Want to be truly amazing? When seeking the spotlight, never, ever forget that every spotlight has an operator.

70

Leaders often wonder how to create a culture of engagement where people really give of themselves to their teammates and to their organizations, particularly during difficult times. What is the secret? The secret is: there is no one big thing. It's all the little things that leaders and team members do every day that add up.

Amazing leaders ask themselves, "What small thing did I do yesterday to support and recognize my team's efforts?" Answer that question daily and you'll be having a greater impact on your team than you can imagine.

Hat tip: Sandi Coryell, The Coryell Group, www.thecoryellgroup.com

71

I'll never forget the moment I first saw Saturn in a telescope. It was a 3-inch refractor that I had gotten for my tenth birthday. As I sat in the front yard I thought, "This must surely be as good as the telescope Galileo had, and he saw Saturn's rings. I wonder…"

When I saw it, I was amazed. Awestruck. I could barely believe it was real. That little dot in the sky really had a ring around it. It looked like a tiny little sculpture floating in my eyepiece.

The pictures that had come back from Voyager 1 and Voyager 2 were enormous investments. The mission, the probes, the experiments, and those photos were built on the educations of hundreds of people and procured at great expense by the American taxpayer. Yet for all their costs, they had suddenly become secondary to my own personal experience through a beat-up garage sale telescope with a busted tripod leg and no finder scope.

No matter how sophisticated your audience's expectations based on other people's reports, they will ultimately become secondary to the actual experience you deliver. It doesn't matter how simple the delivery, as long as the experience is amazing.

72

Will trumps distraction, whim, and instinct. Your will is greater than your want.

Amazing is an act of will.

73

"Who could ask for anything more?"
— Ethel Merman, "I Got Rhythm"

"Please, sir — I want some more."
— Oliver Twist

"Life's a banquet and most poor suckers are starving to death."
— Mame Dennis

Ethel Merman was the biggest voice on Broadway, but if you apply this thinking to your business, you're putting a limit on what you can do for yourself and your audience.

Like Oliver, you too can ask for more. The amazing truth is that no matter what you have or have not yet achieved, there is more. Ask for it – ask yourself, ask God, ask your friends and associates. Ask for the next connection. Brainstorm the next idea. The work continues.

Auntie Mame had it right. Don't miss the banquet.

74

You know that saying, "If it were easy, everyone would do it?" That's wishful thinking. Many people don't or won't even do the easy stuff.

You can choose to amaze by doing the easy stuff well. The things you know should be done but aren't doing. Following up. Reaching out. Planning. Executing.

It's not so hard to do *one* easy task, but it is certainly a challenge to do *all* the easy tasks.

It's still amazing to do the easy stuff well.

75

Magicians and mentalists have long been conscious of an uneasy truth: the secrets to the amazing illusions we perform are nowhere near as impressive as the audience likes to imagine. Part of the reason we keep the secrets is because they are often almost embarrassingly mundane. And yet, put together in the right combination, they create amazing experiences for our audiences.

Sure, some people have exceptional gifts that we find amazing. But the power to amaze isn't limited to those with such gifts; you can be amazing with things you already know how to do if they are combined in ways that lead to unexpected and delightful results.

Your amazing results often lie in a creative and unique combination of the familiar skills you take for granted.

76

*"Most of the important things in the world
have been accomplished by people who have kept on trying
when there seemed to be no hope at all."*
– Dale Carnegie

*"Good times and bum times, I've seen 'em all and my dear,
I'm still here.
Plush velvet sometimes, sometimes just pretzels and beer.
But I'm here."*
– Stephen Sondheim, "Follies"

Surviving, whether on determined grit or pure stubbornness, is still amazing to a world accustomed to giving up. Choose persistence.

It's not just the strong who survive. It's the amazing.

77

Amazement is a delightful and profound emotional state. We feel it when things occur that transcend our expectations of what is possible.

As our skills, technology, and expectations increase, we seem to feel true amazement less frequently. There was a time when looking up the answer to a question required an encyclopedia or a trip to the library. Now you can answer nearly any random question in the world with your phone while sitting on a beach watching the surf.

Magicians and mentalists know that to expose the secret behind an amazing experience isn't just a theatrical let-down. It ultimately robs the audience of a rare and delicate emotion.

When you amaze your audience, don't rob them of their amazement by discussing the details of the method. Let the experience do the talking.

78

"Pick a card, put it back, and the magician finds it," is probably the most familiar plot in card magic. Yet people are still amazed by variations on this theme; in my work I regularly get gasps of amazement with techniques that were already old when my grandparents were born.

In an iPad era, why can people still be amazed by the execution of moves and sequences designed a century ago? Because there's no substitute for a *live* performance comprised of technical *excellence* and a *compelling* narrative framework.

Mind your PQS: Presence. Quality. Story.

79

In magic, the overall context in which an illusion is experienced can heighten the impact of the effect. Making a ham sandwich appear out of thin air in your stage show may be impressive. Making a ham sandwich appear out of thin air when someone says she's hungry – that's amazing. It's relevant and meaningful at that precise moment.

Max Malini, one of history's great magicians well worth your trip to Wikipedia, would go to great lengths just to *prepare* to amaze someone. He would then wait – he would even "vait a veek" if needed – in order to produce the surprise at just the right moment.

What surprise are you holding in reserve for just the right moment for your audience? Have you got an amazing experience that doesn't happen every time, but is there in case the perfect moment should arise?

Legends are born from such audience experiences.

80

Intensity, focus, and drive are amazing characteristics for individual excellence as well as corporate or team performance. All other things being equal, those qualities tend to win the day. All other things being unequal, those qualities tend to equalize them.

People and teams of amazing character invest in developing those amazing characteristics.

81

The performing arts genre of musical theatre is often mocked as corny, unrealistic, and old-fashioned. (Magic is similarly derided, which means I personally endure a double dose of built-in corn, but that's a different story.) The distinctive and most-ridiculed feature of musical theatre is that characters will burst into song – not randomly, as often said, but when the emotion and message rise to a point where mere dialogue is insufficient.

If you want to be amazing, your goal is to lead your audience to a place where their normal means of expression is inadequate. Out of an abundance of emotion – in this case, amazement – they will want to let it out somehow.

If you achieve your mission – amazing them to a point where they feel compelled to express it – then your next job is to tell them how to express it. You give them the script for the next step: sign up for a newsletter, post a photo or comment on a social media page, write an online review, call the radio station… whatever it is.

When they have to burst into song, make sure it's the song you wrote for precisely that moment!

82

Want to be more amazing? Hang out with people more amazing than you are and be open to their honest, constructive criticism.

83

Change your voice mail greeting to create an unexpected moment of delight for your client. What interaction do you want to have with them? Your greeting should help them begin that conversation.

Hat tip: Toni Newman; Attract, Keep and Engage More Customers; www.toninewman.com

84

Shared visions are something of a myth. You cannot precisely share another person's vision any more than you can share their actual eyeball. Values can be shared, but visions cannot. The vision varies from person to person, even when they use the same words to describe it. This is because a person's vision includes an element of the impact it has on them personally.

Amazing leaders realize that ultimately, you don't inspire people to act on your vision. You inspire people to act on their own vision of their participation in whatever you propose as a leader.

A shared vision, then, isn't a giant statue that you sculpt for everyone else to see, or a giant battery that you charge up and others plug into. It is the sum of congruent individual visions that a leader has aligned by communicating value.

How are you communicating the values that will help your audience identify how their vision is congruent with yours? That is the key to amazing leadership.

85

If you want to have an amazing impact on people, train yourself to remember their names. No excuses, no "I just have a problem remembering names." You can take action right now to improve your memory for names as well as other information, and you don't have to take my workshop in order to do it.

Some time ago, I posted an easy technique for improving your memory for names on my blog. Just search Google for "How to Remember Names – the Memory Mojo Way" and you'll find it easily.

Alternately, you can search out any of several books on mnemonic memory training by Harry Lorayne, the famous close-up magician and renowned memory trainer. Some of them can even be found for free online.

Your influence and effectiveness will skyrocket.

86

Personal character is like a skyscraper. It is slow, difficult and usually costly to build. It is a giant beacon to others, towering visibly among the others around it.

Unfortunately, it is almost trivially easy, fast, and cheap to tear a skyscraper down once the demolition crew has been given access to the structure.

Who or what has access to your structure? Are they maintaining it or are they placing charges that will detonate sometime in the future?

Amazing people maintain their skyscrapers.

87

The biggest hindrance to my personal development has not been a function of external circumstances. My biggest hindrance has been my own ego.

The inability to honestly invite, accept, and process legitimate criticism stands in the way of improvement. That may be caused by either a deflated or an inflated ego. You may think you are too bad to ever improve, or you may think you are too good to need it.

The amazing person has a healthy ego. "I am uniquely valuable to the world, and I can grow to be even moreso."

88

Amazing people seem to have an ability to motivate others to accomplish goals. That ability is somewhat illusory, because you cannot motivate someone to want for your reason what they do not want for their own reason.

Amazing motivators are really amazing communicators who help others discover and understand their own reasons for wanting to take action.

89

Put an inexpensive power strip in your laptop case and you'll be an amazing hero at the crowded coffee shop.

For bonus amazing points, leave it there for others to use after you have gone.

90

Disappointment and discouragement are natural reactions to the realization that a desired outcome will not be met. These are weighty emotions, heavy with quiet introspection over what more might have been done and pensive grief over what might have been the result.

In the midst of the grief, amazing people remember that weight can have its uses. Weight can drag, but it can also be used to exert force. It can be placed on a lever to move objects. It may provide an essential boost to the power of your catapult.

Don't ignore the weight of disappointment. Channel it into useful application toward a thoughtful goal.

91

Good people have a knack for forgiving others. Amazing people have learned to extend that same grace to themselves.

Hat tip: Shirley Elmendorf, "Your Best You," www.yourbestyoulifecoaching.com

92

Sure, there is always somebody out there somewhere who is smarter, better funded, better connected, more experienced, more talented, or better looking than you.

Fortunately, they are almost never around.

Get busy.

93

Amazing leaders do not neglect the importance of sustaining their organization's culture. The founding stories, the crucial decision points, the influence of key people, even the blooper reel… the fabric of your culture is woven from these stories. That fabric is prone to wear; it must be rewoven regularly.

Want to have an amazing impact in an organization, either as a leader or as a team member? Capture the cultural legends in a useful form that can be shared with others as they join the group. Don't lose your legends.

94

Never underestimate the amazing value of a short afternoon power-nap on your personal and professional effectiveness. Besides the recharging benefits, it also provides you with the opportunity to take a fresh look at whatever issues are on your plate.

If your office environment allows, or even if you can manage a trip to your car, twenty minutes of eyes-closed, mind-cleared, unplugged rest can be a game-changer.

95

One indicator that an amazing interaction is occurring is that time seems to pass more quickly. Amazing books, plays, or movies that are very long in absolute terms may seem to be over surprisingly soon in perceived time.

The degree of engagement in an interaction is a virtual speedometer for how quickly time will seem to pass as it happens. If you ever thought time travel was amazing, you were right – just for a different reason than you expected!

96

Amazing people tend to ask more questions than others. An instinctive curiosity is not just a pathway to continuous learning; it is a constant reminder of the limits of your current knowledge.

Cultivate curiosity in yourself and others. Look for the assumptions and rules of thumb… and the reasons, if any, behind them.

97

It's fun to be amazing, but it's an impractical waste of amazingness not to be sharing it with others.

You can garner more amazing publicity and PR for your brand by looking weekly at the top news stories and connecting your expertise to that story in some way. This approach works not just for press releases, but also for generating content on your social media platforms.

98

Amazing performers know that they have to choose wardrobe that "pops" so that they can be seen in front of whatever is behind them. Magicians know that this principle can be used to draw attention to what they wish the audience to see, while allowing other details to fade unnoticed into the background.

Take a tip from the show-biz world. Choose to make your strengths and differentiators "pop" in relation to the way others frame themselves and communicate with others. Contrast is the key to visibility.

99

The bank of elevators in a building I visit regularly was recently renovated with a more efficient floor selection process. Instead of selecting a floor once you board an elevator, you choose your floor on a keypad in the hallway. The display screen tells you which car to board and programs it to stop on your floor.

The result? You rarely have cars that stop on every floor; in fact, you often get an express trip. Everyone enjoys faster trips and shorter wait times, all due to the process of clarifying everyone's destination in advance, during a part of the overall process that was previously wasted time.

What parts of your process are simply wasted "wait time?" That part of your process may hold the key to a quantum leap in your audience's experience. Amazing leaders don't wait until everyone boards to figure out where everyone's going.

100

When we think of what it means to encourage or discourage someone, we generally think in terms of being or not being rather vaguely supportive of that person's activities. Rarely, though, do we think of it in terms of the actual root of the word: courage.

At its core, to encourage someone really means you are creating a more courageous person by your words and actions.

The amazing encourager transcends mere support; they are creating courage in others!

101

The act of amazing your audience is like a performing art. It requires dedication, practice, rehearsal, and especially… an audience.

No matter how great the actor, he does not experience the play in the way an audience does. That alternate world doesn't really come into existence until there is an audience to experience it. Without them, it's just another dress rehearsal.

It is important to love practicing and rehearsing, but you love them like you love your sister.

The romance, however, is with the audience.

AMAZING NETWORKING

*A collection of common-sense tips
for shining at meetings and networking events*

There are a variety of networking meetings and events where people can go to increase visibility, meet potential customers, and grow their networks. Here are some tips that will help you avoid looking like you have no idea what you're doing in a meeting of professionals.

Etiquette and Elevator Speeches

When you go to a networking event, remember that the people at the event are not your prospects. They are your gatekeepers. You are not there to make them into your customers; you are there to transform them into your sales force.

Don't go in hoping to sell to the people around you. Think about the kinds of people they may know or interact with. Who might be on their email lists or in their contacts? Sure, you'll do some business with the people you meet, but your goal is to create business for them and for yourself by putting your networks together.

Here's the real truth: most people at a professional networking meeting do not actually care about your product or service no matter how revolutionary it is. This goes for your pill, dietary supplement, exercise program, amazing card trick, electric skin zapper, fruit juice, health product, or any other cool thing that you have or do. They care about *their* cool things that *they* have or do. You have to break through this by being clear, specific, and interesting.

If you get a chance to make a 30 or 60 second speech, make it pithy, memorable, and focused on helping attendees connect you to other people they know. Don't tell the people in the room how long you've been in business. Don't tell them why you think they should buy your product or why they should even be excited about it. Don't say your target market is "everyone" or "anyone." In your short speech, tell them who you are and what you do. Tell them the specific types of clients that you are looking to meet – describe your best clients in the last 6-12 months. And tell them how you would want them to describe your business if telling others about it. Be charming, grateful, confident, and bold. Speak up so you can be heard.

Cell Phones

Set your phone on vibrate or turn it off. When it rings and you reach down to turn it off, most people will politely say, "Oh, that's okay." They are lying. It is not okay – everyone there is, in fact, disturbed that your phone went off and interrupted whomever was speaking at that moment. Even if their own phone rang earlier, they are still ticked at you. Put your phone on vibrate or turn it off. Keep it off the table where it will rattle the whole table. Put it in a pocket, hold it in your lap, put it in your purse, or just turn it off. You may need to be contacted during the meeting – that's fine. Your task as a competent, considerate networker is to find a way to be discreet.

If you must take a call, don't answer it until you are out of the room. If your phone does go off and you must take the call, don't answer it as you are standing up to exit. Yes, it is 10% considerate of you to excuse yourself to take the call, but it is 90% inconsiderate of you to begin it with "Hello? Uh, I'm in a meeting – let me step out" as you step over and around and through chairs to get to the door. If you don't want to drop the call, click the answer button on the way out, but don't speak until you have actually left the room. They'll hear that you're moving and wonder what is going on, but you don't say a word. If they hang up before you can answer or speak, you can call them back in the hallway.

Microphones

If there is a microphone, use it. Yes, use it even if you don't want to. Yes, use it even if you have a loud voice and you think it carries well. Yes, use it even if over the course of your entire life, everyone has told you that you don't need it. They are wrong.

If there is a microphone there and it's working, you need to use it. It makes weaker voices strong enough to be heard. It makes stronger voices even more understandable. It helps to give your voice authority and pop that help people to pay attention. If others are using it and you don't, then the whole feel of the meeting changes unnecessarily. Most people don't use a microphone because they are afraid of what their voice sounds like when amplified. Get over it. Use the microphone.

Hold the microphone closer to your mouth. Just because you are holding it doesn't magically make you heard. You can't hold it at your chest or a foot away from your mouth – you actually have to speak into it for it to work properly. Hold the microphone about 5 inches from your mouth and speak into it. It's okay if you're louder than the person before you. He didn't know how to use it properly and now you do. Don't gesture with it, point at other things with it, or wave it at other people. If you need to gesture, use your other hand.

Don't grip the microphone at the very bottom. Many wireless microphones have their transmitting hardware in that area. Grasp the microphone around the middle of the barrel.

Nametags

Nametags are traditionally worn on the right side of the body so that they are most visible during your first handshake. This is a rule of thumb and while you may be coached on this by some networking veterans, don't sweat this too much.

The rear-adhesive nametags are notorious for falling off easily. Here's a handy tip: keep a couple of paper clips in the car. If you affix your tag to a part of your clothing near an edge (lapel, collar, ruffle, etc.) then you can slide the clip on to help it stay in place.

More experienced networkers have probably moved into having a custom name badge produced, typically with a magnetic clip so that you don't have to pin through your clothes. Here's a tip: many events feature plastic name badges which have magnetic clips. You can probably keep one from the next event you attend, then create your own custom badge on a printer and just drop it in. Make your name large enough to be seen in a dim room, and include a QR code of your contact information or a link to your social media site of choice.

Food and Beverage

There are multiple philosophies on eating and drinking at networking events. Some people say you shouldn't do it at all, while others say it's no big deal. My view is that it is a function of how productive you want the meeting to be, and whether you already have an established presence at that organization.

If this is your first visit to that organization and you don't know many people, I suggest you eat before you arrive or wait until afterward. Spend your time meeting as many people as possible. You want to walk away with at least a dozen people whose businesses you've learned something about, who have learned something about your business, and who have given you permission to contact them on social media. You want to make a great impression on these people; crumbs on your tie will not help.

If you've become a regular at the event and already know most folks who attend, then eating is a different consideration. I suggest getting there early and enjoying your snack, then dive in with networking the rest of the time.

If you have two free hands while other people have

one or none, then you will have the opportunity to be extremely helpful to other people during the event. Maximize this opportunity to make a great impression.

There is often alcohol available at after-hours events. You don't need another lecture on the dumb and/or dangerous things that can happen when you drink too much. Make wise choices.

Professional Image

Choose your attire with some forethought. People will judge your business capabilities by the way you look, the way you talk, the way you behave, and the overall impression you make as a human being. Your business is not a business card or a contract or a corporate seal. It is not even a name or a logo. At a networking event, your business is you, personally. Your face, your hair, your clothes, your hygiene, and your manners.

Nobody said it was fair or accurate for your entire business to be judged by those things. I'm just telling you that your personal impression is the first experience that people will have with your brand.

I keep a container of breath mints in my car, as well as nail clippers, a hairbrush, some tweezers, a lint brush, and skin moisturizer. In some cases, I may even bring my electric shaver with me so that I can clean up before an after-hours event.

The business impact is both immediate and long-lasting. If you have created an impressive personal and professional image – one with which others would be proud to be associated – then you can charge more for your services. Furthermore, the perceived value of what you do will increase. Here's a lesson to remember: if the audience perceives your value is higher, then your REAL value to your client is higher. I regularly get paid to do the very same events that others would have to do for free "for the exposure." This is not by accident.

Don't look like a rumpled slob when you go out to network or get in front of people at a leads meeting or other meeting. Clean up. You may not need to wear a suit and tie, but you need to present yourself in a way consistent with the value you propose to deliver.

If you engage in professional networking, people will talk about you later. Hopefully they will be talking about the great impression you made and how you have an amazing way of presenting your business. Don't distract them from that task by giving them negative things to talk about in terms of your personal and professional appearance, your etiquette, or your ability to be heard and understood.

HIGH JOELTAGE!

JOE M. TURNER

Photo by Teryl Jackson | www.terylphoto.com

ABOUT THE AUTHOR

Joe M. Turner is an author, speaker, and multi-talented corporate entertainer based in Atlanta, Georgia.

Even while successfully climbing the ladder as a change management specialist in a global consulting firm, Joe never abandoned his deep skills in the performing arts including piano and vocal music, theatre, and illusion arts, especially sleight-of-hand magic and mentalism. He ultimately combined his performing talents with his business experience to create a new business and an exciting new career.

Now Joe speaks and entertains at conferences and other events across America as well as internationally. Using magic and illusion as a tool for engagement, entertainment, and communication, he presents keynotes and after-dinner programs all over the world as "The Chief Impossibility Officer."

Joe and his wife Rosemary are the proud parents of Hayley and Preston. You can connect with Joe online at www.turnermagic.com, as well as on Facebook and LinkedIn. Follow Joe on Twitter at @turnermagic - and expect to see the occasional *#hailstate* in his tweets.

www.turnermagic.com

Made in the USA
Columbia, SC
06 June 2025